To DSL and SAL, who grew up on Debbie's music, and to SHL, who encouraged me and tried his best to sing her songs —E.L.

KAR-BEN PUBLISHING®
An imprint of Lerner Publishing Group, Inc.
241 First Avenue North
Minneapolis, MN 55401 USA

Website address: www.karben.com

Back matter photos provided by Debbie Friedman's family.
Main body text set in Aptifer Slab LT pro.
Typeface provided by Lynotype AG.

Library of Congress Cataloging-in-Publication Data

Names: Leventhal, Ellen, 1951– author. | Grebtsova, Natalia, illustrator.
Title: Debbie's song : the Debbie Friedman story / Ellen Leventhal ; illustrated by Natalia Grebtsova.
Description: Minneapolis : Kar-Ben Publishing ®, 2023. | Audience: Ages 3–8 | Audience: Grades 2–3 | Summary: "Debbie Friedman always had music inside of her, and she had a dream. She thought music could heal the world and bring people closer. She did something radical and new-created Jewish music that brings the whole Jewish community together"— Provided by publisher.
Identifiers: LCCN 2022015403 (print) | LCCN 2022015404 (ebook) | ISBN 9781728443010 (library binding) | ISBN 9781728443027 (paperback) | ISBN 9781728480923 (ebook)
Subjects: LCSH: Friedman, Debbie—Juvenile literature. | Jewish composers—Biography—Juvenile literature.
Classification: LCC ML410.F89 G74 2023 (print) | LCC ML410.F89 (ebook) | DDC 780.89/924—dc23/eng/20220331

LC record available at https://lccn.loc.gov/2022015403
LC ebook record available at https://lccn.loc.gov/2022015404

Manufactured in the United States of America
1-50144-49813-5/18/2022

DEBBIE'S SONG

The Debbie Friedman Story

Ellen Leventhal

illustrated by Natalia Grebtsova

KAR-BEN
PUBLISHING

When Debbie Friedman was a little girl, music bubbled up inside her.

ALL the time.

Notes and melodies.

Loud and quiet.

Fast and slow.

All swirling around inside her, just waiting to burst out.

It was her superpower.

Debbie loved singing—especially with her bubbe.

As Debbie sang the blessings over the Shabbat candles, the world seemed brighter.

When Debbie was six, she and her family moved halfway across the country, from New York to Minnesota.

Far away from her grandparents.

Away from Bubbe,

from Zayde,

from the life she knew.

But still, her love of music

bubbled,

rumbled,

and tumbled inside her.

Debbie's music made people happy.

As Debbie grew up, she became a song leader at Jewish summer camps. There she sang, laughed, and even taught herself to play guitar!

Debbie couldn't read music, but that didn't stop her. Over and over she'd practice . . .

plink,

plink,

plink . . .

until she got the chords and melodies just right.

After high school, Debbie's fierce spirit and love of Judaism led her to a kibbutz in Israel. There, adults and children lived, prayed, worked, and sang together.

For six months, Debbie enjoyed life on the kibbutz. But returning home,
she found herself sitting in the synagogue twiddling her thumbs,

fidgeting and fussing,

staring and wondering.

Why were people sitting,

with their arms crossed,

apart,

silent?

She glanced up at the bimah
and saw only serious faces.
Young people sat in the pews
and stared with blank faces.

Where was the joy?

Surrounded by people, Debbie felt alone.

It was NOT right.

She remembered her time on the kibbutz:

everyone working and playing,

singing and praying—together.

She closed her eyes and pictured Bubbe, Zayde, and her mother healing the whole world with their good acts every day.

Her music itched to get out, and she wondered:

Could I heal the world with my music? Could I use music to bring people closer?

She imagined people singing together—as a community—and a dream formed.

She would create community.

Ideas spun inside her like a tornado.

She would use her superpower to write Jewish music that would

welcome,

include,

and honor

the voices of everyone!

No one had ever done that in the world of Jewish music, and Debbie knew it would not be easy. She was just one person with a new idea.

But something else rumbled inside her.

Determination.

One day Debbie hopped on a bus, and as it bounced along, a wonderful new melody formed in her head.

If she wanted to make Jewish music that everyone could sing, she needed words.

"I've never written lyrics," she thought.

But that didn't stop her.

Debbie started by translating a prayer.

A few weeks later, she taught that song to a group of teenagers, and—WOW!

They sang loud, beautiful music.

Not music they heard on the radio.

And not music they heard in school.

Or even at summer camp.

A prayer with words and a melody that EVERYONE could sing rose into the air.

The teens linked arms and swayed to the music.

Tears trickled down their faces, and Debbie's eyes sparkled with excitement.

Soon, words began bubbling up inside her and pushing to get out.

Big words,

    little words,

        Hebrew words,

           and English words.

Debbie wove the English and Hebrew words together like a tapestry.

The simple chords and easily sung lyrics welcomed everyone,
even those who didn't know Hebrew.

Nobody felt alone with Debbie's new music.

She wrote for those who felt different,

for those who felt left out,

for young children,

and for herself.

Debbie's songs soared across the country and landed in big cities and small towns, tearing down barriers that separated people.

But not everyone liked her songs.

They made some people angry.

"We need traditional Jewish music, just as we've always had!"

"She's not trained in Jewish music!"

"She can't even read music!"

For Debbie, it was like riding a twisty roller coaster.

Up, up, up, she'd climb, knowing she was making many people happy—

but the grumbling continued,

and . . . WHOOSH!

Down,

down,

down she'd slide,

landing with an unhappy *THUMP!*

Many people laughed at her ideas about how prayers could be sung and what kinds of Jewish songs belonged in synagogues.

Others said mean things.

Some turned their backs on her.

But Debbie knew the world needed her music.

She refused to bottle up the songs bubbling inside her.

Her music rippled out into the world, and soon its joyful sound was heard everywhere—in Jewish summer camps and schools, and even in synagogues.

VISIT ISRAEL

One night, Debbie found herself in Carnegie Hall, one of the most famous concert halls in the world.

She stepped onto the stage, and the audience exploded with excitement, waiting to hear her songs, clapping and cheering.

In front of a packed audience, Debbie's music soared all the way up to the high ceiling,

bouncing against the walls,

cascading throughout the room.

When Debbie lifted her arms, inviting the audience to join her, hundreds of voices filled the huge hall.

Debbie's songs lifted the audience.

And like magic, a group of strangers became a community.

Just as Debbie dreamed they would.

About Debbie Friedman

Deborah Lynn Friedman continued to sing long after her first appearance at Carnegie Hall. She became one of the most influential and respected singer-songwriters of Jewish music in the world. She recorded more than twenty albums, selling half a million copies across the globe. But more important, Debbie Friedman changed the way people related to Judaism. She broke barriers and touched people's lives.

Debbie, at the age of 2 or 3

Debbie with her mom on the back steps of the family home on Baker Avenue in Utica, New York

Debbie included women's voices and stories in such songs as "L'chi Lach" and "Miriam's Song." She also wrote for children, who loved singing along to her simple rhythms and fun songs such as "The Aleph Bet Song" and "The Latke Song." But Debbie is probably best known for her rendition of the "Mi Shebeirach," a prayer of healing sung in synagogues across the world. Not only did her music make prayer more accessible to millions, but her determination to succeed inspired many young people to go after their dreams.

Debbie was born on February 23, 1951, in Utica, New York, and moved with her parents and two sisters to St. Paul, Minnesota, when she was six.

Debbie had a passion for all types of music but was primarily influenced by folk singers of her time, such as Joan Baez and Peter, Paul, and Mary. And like them, she used her voice to challenge those in positions of power.

She did not have rabbinic or cantorial training. When some people accused her of wanting to get rid of tradition, she explained that there was room for everyone and for all types of Jewish music in Jewish liturgy.

Debbie served as the cantorial soloist at the New Reform Congregation in Los Angeles in the 1980s. She sat on faculties dealing with end-of-life care, Jewish education, spiritual renewal, and much more. After being seen as an outsider for many years, in 2007, Debbie was appointed

Debbie (*right*) with sister Cheryl

Debbie at the beginning of her singing career in the early 1970s

to the faculty at Hebrew Union College-Jewish Institute of Religion's School of Sacred Music, the school for Reform rabbis and cantors.

At the age of thirty-seven, Debbie began to suffer from a neurological condition. Although often in pain and no longer able to perform her trademark clapping and foot stomping, Debbie kept going. When people told her how amazing she was, Debbie made it clear that they too had special gifts.

After Debbie died in 2011, Hebrew Union College renamed the cantorial school program the Debbie Friedman School of Sacred Music.

Glossary

bimah (BEE-mah): a podium from which the Torah is read and services are led in a synagogue

bubbe (BUH-bee): the Yiddish word for grandmother

cantor (CAN-tor): a Jewish clergyperson who sings liturgical music and leads prayer

kibbutz (kih-BOOTS): a settlement, often a farm, where everything is shared by the whole community, located in Israel

Shabbat (shuh-BAHT): the Jewish Sabbath, which begins at sundown on Friday night and continues until sundown on Saturday

synagogue (SIN-uh-gog): a Jewish house of worship

zayde (ZAY-dee): the Yiddish word for grandfather

Author's Note

Not long before I started writing this book, I walked the halls of a Jewish elementary school, and I heard music coming from one of the classrooms. The children were singing Debbie Friedman's "L'chi Lach." I smiled, thinking about the time I met Debbie very briefly and about the many hours I sang her songs with my children and my students.

When the children got to the line "And you shall be a blessing," I thought about Debbie herself, and I began to think about writing a picture book about her. I promptly went home and contacted Debbie's sister, Cheryl Friedman, who has been invaluable to me as I attempted to craft Debbie's story.

Talking to people about their memories of Debbie connected me to her. Everyone took Debbie into their hearts in their own way, but her love of Judaism, music, and people shone through each interview. I especially want to thank Rabbi Samuel Karff of blessed memory, who was instrumental in helping Debbie start her career, as well as Liz Karff Seitz, Cantor Star Trompeter, Gay Block, and of course, Cheryl Friedman for sharing their memories with me.

It would be challenging to include all of Debbie Friedman's accomplishments in a picture book and impossible to name the thousands of people she has touched. But that's not the object of this book. Aside from letting young readers into Debbie's world, I hope Debbie's story inspires them to go after their dreams and stand up for what they believe. That is Debbie's legacy.

And she shall be a blessing.

About the Author

Ellen Leventhal is an educator and writer in Houston, Texas. She taught in a Jewish school where Debbie Friedman's music could be heard as she walked down the hallways. Ellen is the author of several picture books as well as short stories and poetry. Her favorite thing to do is visit schools and share her love of literacy and the importance of having a dream. To learn more about Ellen, go to www.EllenLeventhal.com.

About the Illustrator

Natalia Grebtsova draws digitally to create amazing worlds. She is inspired by her love of nature and animals. Her nickname is "Belouhaya Marmozetka," which means "White-Eared Marmoset." She lives in Moscow, Russia.